The Littlest
Book of Small Things

Edited by Janet Shirley

with colour illustrations

by Bernhard Oberdieck

Ragged Bears

He that contemneth small things shall fall by little and little.

Ecclesiasticus

What a large volume of adventures may be grasped within this little span of life by him who interests his heart in everything.

Laurence Sterne

Some have too much, yet still do crave;
  I little have and seek no more.
They are but poor though much they have,
  And I am rich with little store.

Edward Dyer

Remember little kindnesses and forget small faults.

Chinese proverb

I would go to a covert
    Where the birds sing;
Where in the whitethorn
    Singeth a thrush,
And a robin sings
    In the holly bush.
Full of fresh scents
    Are the budding boughs
Arching high over
    A cool green house.

        Christina Rossetti

It has long been an axiom of mine that the little things are infinitely the most important.

Arthur Conan Doyle

You need to look at what the Spring is doing
Putting forth little treasures, primroses and
the like.

. . . .

You must take care of all that life has given,
And keep it gratefully.

Margaret Cropper

A pennyweight of love is worth a pound of law.

Proverb

Freckled nest eggs shalt thou see
Hatching in the hawthorn tree,
When the hen-bird's wing doth rest
Quiet on her mossy nest.

John Keats

Bright-winged insects on the flowers of May
Shine pearls too wealthy to be cast away.

John Clare

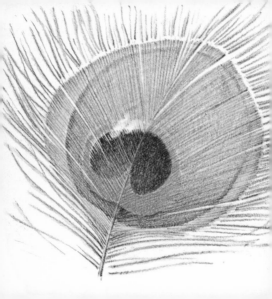

A lily of a day
Is fairer far in May,
Although it fall and die that night;
It was the plant and flower of light.
In small proportions we just beauties see;
And in short measures life may perfect be.

Ben Jonson

The world is full of small joys, but you must learn to see them.

Li Tai-Pe

The pride of the peacock is the glory of God.

William Blake

Is it so small a thing
To have enjoyed the sun,
To have lived light in the spring,
To have loved, to have thought, to have done?

Matthew Arnold

Reprint 1992

© 1989 ars edition, CH-6301 Zug in association with
Ragged Bears Ltd., Andover, Hampshire
All rights reserved · Printed in Germany
ISBN 1 870817 09 5

The Littlest Books Collection

The Littlest Christmas Book
The Littlest Easter Bunny Book
The Littlest Book Just for You
The Littlest Book for Every Day
The Littlest Book for a Friend
The Littlest Book for the Heart
The Littlest Book for a Joyful Event
The Littlest Book for Mother's Day
The Littlest Book of Bears
The Littlest Book of Birds
The Littlest Book of Ireland
The Littlest Book of Kittens
The Littlest Book of Mice
The Littlest Book of Monet's Garden
The Littlest Book of Scotland
The Littlest Book of Trees
The Littlest Book of Venice
The Littlest Book of the
12 Days of Christmas